Common Practices for Country Risk Management

in U.S. Banks

Interagency Country Exposure Review Committee
Country Risk Management Sub-Group

November 1998

Common Practices for Country Risk Management in U.S. Banks
November 1998

Contents

Page

Background

The bank regulatory agencies decided in fourth quarter 1997 to review the country risk management processes used by U.S. banks to verify information and update examination guidance.

In October 1997 and March 1998, Interagency Country Exposure Review Committee (ICERC) examiners from the OCC, Federal Reserve, and FDIC collected information informally on the country risk management processes employed by a sample of multinational, regional, and smaller banks involved in the ICERC country risk discussion process.

A set of questions (Attachment) on various areas of country risk management was developed by the agencies to guide those examiners in their collection efforts. This information was collected solely in the regular examinations of the banks.

Purpose

This paper is intended to provide examiners and bankers with a better understanding of the variety of approaches used in U.S. banks to measure, monitor, and control country risk exposures. Information collected is not intended to depict the complete spectrum of country risk management processes used in the U.S. banking system, nor to set forth minimum regulatory requirements for country risk management processes. However, when possible, the paper identifies common elements in the country risk management process elements that should be considered by examiners during the examination of individual banks.

This paper consists of an Executive Summary of Common Attributes of Country Risk Management, followed by sections discussing country risk management processes under the headings multinational banks, regional banks, and small banks.

EXECUTIVE SUMMARY

Overall Conclusion

Country risk management processes and practices vary significantly among U.S. banks. Although some general similarities can be identified, large differences exist in how the banks identify, measure, set limits for, monitor, and manage country risk exposures.

Nonetheless, the ICERC's informal survey identified the following common attributes of existing country risk management processes.

Country Risk Management Process and Policies

X   All banks have developed formal country risk management programs. Most programs are centralized.

X   Banks usually have adopted formal country risk management policies that are board approved.

X   All banks have formal internal country risk monitoring and reporting mechanisms. The type and content of country risk management reporting to senior management, board-appointed committees, and the board of directors vary considerably.

X   Typically, country risk management is integrated with credit risk management. However, several large banks integrate country risk management into their overall risk management process.

X   Responsibility for country risk management generally lies with either a senior country risk officer or a high-level country risk committee.

X   Most bank country managers are responsible for recommending specific country marketing strategies and risk tolerances.

X   Several multinational and regional banks have established procedures to deal with deteriorating country risk situations. But, the most common practice relies on informal communication lines between experienced managers in times of crisis.

Country Risk Analysis

X   Most banks maintain formal country risk analysis files at headquarters and supplemental files in foreign branches.

X   The contents of country risk files vary considerably. The most common components of country risk files are: internal analysis of political/economic/social issues and risks prepared by country risk officers or international economists; external analysis prepared by rating agencies or consultants; and officer call memos.

X   No multinational or regional bank relies entirely on external country risk analyses. However, several small banks use them as their primary tool to evaluate country risk.

Country Risk Ratings

X   All banks, except for one small institution, assign formal country risk ratings.

X   Most banks' country risk ratings cover a broad definition of country risk, including transfer risk and local currency/indigenous risks.

X   Few multinational banks use country risk ratings that focus solely on transfer risk.

X   Although most banks' country risk ratings definitions appear to parallel ICERC's country ratings, direct correlations are generally unclear. The principal difference is that ICERC's rating definitions focus solely on transfer risk and the banks' definitions on broader country risk issues.

X   Most banks apply country risk ratings to all types of credit and investment risk exposures, including local currency lending.

X   Banks with mainly short-term trade and bank exposures focus on short-term country risk issues versus long-term transfer risk issues.

X   In most banks, country risk ratings are integrated with their commercial credit risk rating system. Generally, country risk ratings establish a ceiling for commercial credit risk ratings (i.e., the borrower's commercial risk rating cannot be better than the country risk rating for its country of domicile).

X   There is wide inconsistency in terms of who has responsibility for assigning country risk ratings. Various alternatives include: a formal country risk committee, an international economics department, the credit department, and country managers.

X   Almost all multinational/regional banks use their commercial ALLL methodology to cover country risk exposures. Few banks also make an extra annual ALLL provision specifically to cover country risk exposures that are criticized or classified internally. Small banks' country risk ALLL allocation processes are less formal. (Note: All U.S. banks must comply with ICERC's specific ATTR determinations for value-impaired-rated countries.)

Country Risk Limits

X   Country risk limits exist in all banks; but they are determined in a variety of ways. Most banks use a "top down" approach that treats the country risk limit as a scarce resource. They factor in the country risk rating. Most large banks use a "value-at-risk" limit for foreign trading accounts. Some banks use a certain percentage of capital as a ceiling for individual country risk limits.

X   Country risk limits generally are approved either by the banks' credit department or country risk committee.

X   Almost all of the banks' country risk limits apply to the broad definition of country risk exposure (i.e., including local currency lending). Two multinational banks' country risk limits apply solely to transfer risk exposures.

X   Few banks have country risk sublimits for insured/uninsured exposures, tenors, and/or types of risk exposure or products.

X   Generally, most banks do not have formal regional concentration or "contagion" limits. However, some banks monitor informally regional concentration exposures for Latin America and Southeast Asia. One multinational bank uses a sophisticated co-variance analysis to set regional limits for "contagion" risk. Several others are developing co-variance models.

X   Almost all banks report country risk limit exceptions to executive management. In addition, many of the banks also report exceptions to the board of directors or its committee.

Multinational Banks

Country Risk Management

Summary Conclusions

X   Country risk generally is integrated with credit risk management under the responsibility of a senior executive or senior management group.

X   Transfer risk, considered a significant risk, is incorporated usually into country risk (i.e., there are generally no separate limits for transfer risk).

X   Most of the multinational banks have a formal country risk monitoring process and some type of reporting to the board of directors. One bank has no specific reporting process.

X   Formal country risk management policies usually are included in the bank's overall credit policy.

X   Country risk management in most banks is centralized; however, few banks have decentralized management and/or credit approval processes.

Responsibility for Country Risk Management

Country risk management generally is centralized under the responsibility of a senior executive level committee or unit. However, two banks' processes, although considered centralized, have a higher degree of de-centralization than most of the other banks. Often those responsible have international lending and credit risk experience.

The process is typically part of credit risk management. The boards of directors are familiar with the country credit risk management process, but most banks do not require annual reporting or review of this process by the board. In all but one bank, there is some level of regular reporting to the board.

Approval of country risk rating and exposure limits is generally the responsibility of a country risk type of committee. Recommendations for ratings and limits are provided by a variety of senior managers and international credit officers. When applicable, input is provided by on-site country managers and credit officers. Normally, only one country risk management committee exists. However, one bank has two committees, one of which is responsible for cross-border exposures and the other for local currency exposures that are self-funded in local currency by its foreign branches and subsidiaries. Another bank also has two committees. One committee is responsible for capital market exposures (liquid short term) and the other for credit exposures. Only one bank has not established a formal country risk management committee.

Reporting Mechanisms and Monitoring

Although all multinational banks monitor country risk, the methods vary. Generally, concentration limits in the form of aggregate country exposure limits and business and product line sublimits are the primary mechanism used to monitor and control country risk. In addition, routine contact is maintained with foreign office managers and credit officers. Often annual visits to the foreign offices are conducted, or the senior country manager and the senior country credit officer makes at least one annual visit to headquarters, at which time they have extensive meetings with senior management. In the interim, senior officers submit periodic reports to the headquarter's business units, international department, and credit department.

The level of reporting varies as well. Three of the banks report the annual aggregate country limits to their board of directors, while one bank did not report to the board. Another bank reported potential country risk problems to the board quarterly, or monthly, if the potential problems were more severe. Aggregate country exposure limits and business and product line sublimits are communicated widely to international business line and credit officers at the country, regional, and headquarters level. One bank reports monthly international exposure and limits covering all types of risk, including local currency exposure, to top level management officials. Another bank reports monthly all exposures to senior management and the board.

Policies and Procedures

Formal policies generally include country risk rating and limits. Most policies are comprehensive. They are found in the bank's credit policy manual and updated periodically. At one bank, the policy became an operational manual, containing additional memos that outlined pertinent policy issues. Generally, the country risk policies and procedures are approved by a country risk committee, comprised of the bank's senior executives and often by the board of directors.

Staffing and Organization

The multinational banks generally have some type of country risk management committee that sets policies and approves country risk ratings and exposure limits and limit and sublimit exceptions. This country risk management committee typically is comprised of headquarters senior executives. For example, the committee can include the chief executive officer, the manager of the international department, the chief credit officer, the senior international credit officer, and the director of the country risk unit.

The banks generally have some type of specialized staff unit within the headquarters international credit department that is responsible for analyzing country risk and preparing the country rating recommendations. This staff unit is comprised of either senior international credit specialists and/or international economists. Discussions with those persons during the ICERC process indicate that their level of expertise and experience is high. Business managers and senior credit officers in a bank's country and/or regional offices contribute information and insights for the country risk analysis, recommend country exposure limits and sublimits, and are responsible for operating within the approved limits and sublimits.

Information on country exposure and sublimit usage is compiled by specialized headquarters operations units that also track and report the bank's exposures by borrower, counterparty, product line, business unit, and industry, etc. In some cases, several bank areas monitor the usage of country exposure limits and sublimits. They can include the headquarters' country risk staff unit, the senior credit officers in each country, and the senior business and product line credit officers in the international department at headquarters. At one bank, the loan review department annually examines all of the larger individual exposures to foreign borrowers and counterparties in its review of exposures for specific product lines or business units. In another bank, the Credit Review Department prepares a special review covering all exposures to borrowers and counterparties in specific emerging market countries. This department is staffed with former senior credit officers with international experience.

Several banks have established specific procedures for monitoring conditions in a deteriorating country. However, most of the banks rely on informal communication lines among experienced managers in times of crisis.

Country Risk Analysis Process

Summary Conclusions

X   All multinational banks conduct a level of internal country risk analysis and subscribe to a variety of external information resources.

X   The majority of the multinational banks have formal country risk files. All banks keep a level of internal and/or external country risk information.

X   Dissemination of analyses is maintained at a senior management level.

Formal Process

Annual internal country risk analyses at most banks generally cover economic, political, and social variables and trends. However, two banks place a much higher emphasis on general economic factors. These analyses are based mostly on internally derived data supplemented by external sources. The analyses often are prepared by a special unit within the International Credit Department. At some banks, the unit consists primarily of international economists, while at others it is composed mainly of experienced senior international credit officers.

Written country risk analyses are required for most foreign countries where banks have credit or capital market exposures. The principal exception to this requirement is that some banks monitor country risk developments, but do not prepare an annual written risk analysis for selected low risk OECD countries (e.g., Germany, United Kingdom).

Upon completion of the annual analyses, most banks will segregate the countries into different categories (e.g., risk classes) based on the level of risk. For "high priority" countries, most banks will perform an in-house analysis. For "low priority" countries, most banks use a combination of external economic, political, and social data, etc.

All of the multinational banks subscribe to two or more external economic research services that provide historic and current economic data and ratio analysis and cover political and social factors and trends. The banks that do not have their own staff of international economists make greater use of the information and base line analyses provided by the external sources. However, none of the banks rely solely on external analyses.

When external information and ratings differ from internal analyses, the differences are discussed by the country risk management committee. No other formal due diligence mechanism was disclosed.

Information Requirements

Most of the multinational banks require formal country risk management files. In the two exceptions, only informal country files are kept. Country credit and/or limit exposures are maintained separately. Generally, the units or persons who prepare the annual risk analyses keep extensive information on each country that can include:

X   Reports from outside economic research services.

X   Published economic data and analysis.

X   Articles from business publications.

X   Situation reports submitted by country managers and credit officers.

X   Call reports from on-site visits by headquarters managers and credit officers.

X   Reports from the major rating agencies.

X   Limit exposure reports.

X   Copies of documentation approving limits, sublimits, and exceptions to limits.

Communication of Analysis/Results

Internally prepared country risk analyses are proprietary. The analyses are distributed typically at a high level and limited to the staff and management of the unit responsible for their preparation, members of the committee that approves the country risk ratings and their staffs, the International Credit Department, the country manager, and senior country credit officer, and for banks that have regional offices, the regional managers and credit officers. Communication at most institutions is on a need-to-know basis.

Country Risk Rating Process

Summary Conclusions

X   All of the multinational banks have a formal country risk rating process.

X   Most banks take a comprehensive view of country risk, but differ on how specific risks (e.g., transfer or sovereign) factor into their country risk rating system. Two banks focus primarily on transfer risk.

X   Many banks apply single country risk ratings to all types of exposure. However, a second rating is used by a few banks for locally funded exposures.

X   Country risk ratings are integrated into credit risk ratings. The country rating usually takes precedence.

X   Most banks' country risk ratings correspond to ICERC. But direct correlations are unclear because ICERC rates only transfer risk, while most banks generally rate overall country risk.

X   Country risk ratings are assigned annually by the responsible governing unit.

X   Validation of country risk ratings is inconsistent in method and depth.

X   ALLL analyses factor in country risk ratings.

Formal Risk Rating Process

Each multinational bank has a formal country risk rating process. Detailed written policies and procedures for analyzing, recommending, and approving country credit risk ratings are usually included in the bank's credit risk policy manual. With one exception, banks prepare and assign annual risk ratings for each country when they have more than a nominal exposure. The exception institution does not assign risk ratings to France, Germany, Japan, Switzerland, and the United Kingdom, because it considers their country risk to be comparable with that of the United States.

Banks generally use their country risk ratings to:

X   Develop the country exposure limits used to manage and monitor aggregate and specific asset country risk, or

X   Adjust the commercial credit risk ratings assigned to individual foreign borrowers, counterparties, and securities issuers by incorporating the country risk.

Banks conduct an interim review and consider assigning a new country rating (between regularly scheduled annual reviews) whenever a potential change occurs in a country's rating. Written policies outline the requirements and procedures for those interim reviews of a country's risk rating.

Covered Risk

Each multinational bank takes a comprehensive view of country risk, but differs in the degree to which they include country specific risks in their country risk rating or in their commercial risk rating system. Banks use either of two general approaches in defining the types of risk covered by their country risk rating. They either define country risk broadly to include all of the country specific economic, political, and social factors that could affect a borrower's ability to repay its obligations, or they limit country risk to a combination of transfer risk and sovereign risk. Two banks' country risk ratings focus primarily on "transfer risk" with the resulting impact on commercial risk ratings.

Every bank, regardless of the approach it chooses, includes transfer risk as a major component of country risk. The basic bank definition of transfer risk is the risk that a country's local currency will not be convertible into a foreign currency, such as US dollars, required for repayment of loans to foreign lenders (i.e., banks). Banks are expanding their definition of transfer risk to include the risk that, due to currency devaluation, borrowers' local currency holdings and cash flow could not be converted into a sufficient quantity of foreign currency to repay their loans to foreign lenders.

The primary measure of transfer risk used by banks is a comparison of the foreign government's ability to meet its external debt obligations from foreign currency reserves, cash flow, credit lines, saleable assets, and its access to new foreign currency loans. These foreign government external debt obligations are defined to include those of state and provincial governments and their agencies, companies owned by national, state, and provincial governments, and third party obligations of private corporations guaranteed by national, state, and provincial governments. Banks are expanding their measurement of a country's transfer risk obligations to include the aggregate cross-border (foreign currency) debt obligations of corporate borrowers. This trend reflects a recognition that some countries use government-approved foreign currency borrowings by corporations to make it appear that, based on their direct government related external debt obligations, they had less transfer risk.

Banks define sovereign risk to include both the ability and willingness of a foreign government to repay its direct and indirect (i.e., guaranteed) foreign currency repayment obligations. Several cases are cited as examples of countries that were able to repay (or refinance) their foreign currency repayment obligations for a period of time, but were unwilling to do so.

Every bank, regardless of which general approach it chooses, includes in its definition of country risk the potential impact of a foreign government's economic, monetary and fiscal policies on the ability of borrowers and counterparties to meet their obligations to the bank.

Covered Exposures and Products

Generally, multinational banks' country risk ratings apply to almost all types of direct and indirect exposures. These can include:

X   Loans to foreign borrowers (commercial, project finance, etc.).

X   Guarantees.

X   Letters of credit.

X   Foreign exchange and derivatives counterparty exposures.

X   Settlement risk.

X   Securities of foreign issuers (whether held in trading, investment or underwriting accounts).

X   Local currency exposures (whether funded with local deposits or US dollars).

X   Direct equity investments, such as the book value of the bank's foreign branches and subsidiaries.

X   Trade finance.

X   Investment banking.

X   Venture capital investments.

One bank will not make a loan to any company without a hard currency repayment source. Another bank=s rating system divides exposures into three major categories: traditional lending with sublimits for trade finance, project finance, and Fed funds; traded derivative products; and tradeable assets, mainly bond positions.

Most of the banks assign a single risk rating to each country that focuses primarily on cross-border credit risk. In addition to on-balance sheet cross-border credit exposures, this single country risk rating is applied directly to:

X   Local currency exposures funded by the bank with U.S. dollar foreign liabilities (i.e., deposits) and subsequently converted into local currency.

X   The on-balance-sheet equivalent value of off-balance-sheet cross-border credit obligations (e.g., derivatives).

X   Any foreign asset valued at its original U.S. dollar cost or book value (e.g., securities held for investment and deposit placements).

Banks recognize that the country risk for local currency exposures funded with local liabilities is less than for cross-border claims because there is no transfer risk. Therefore, a few banks have a second country risk rating that covers local currency exposures (i.e., loans) funded with local currency liabilities (i.e., deposits). However, most banks apply their cross-border country risk rating to their local currency exposures funded with local liabilities, because the same country's specific economic, political, and social factors that would impair a borrower's ability to repay foreign currency obligations, are likely to limit the ability of local currency borrowers to repay their obligations. Or, in some cases, the banks believe that two sets of country risk ratings are too cumbersome. One bank's country risk ratings apply solely to cross-border approval and not to local currency lending.

Integration of Country and Commercial Risk

The country risk rating process is integrated closely with the bank's borrower and counterparty credit risk management function. Most banks use country risk ratings that use the same numerical (i.e., 1 to 10) or rating agency alphabetical risk rating categories (i.e., AAA to B) that the bank uses to assess borrower/counterparty credit risk. Some banks use a single country risk rating category for most countries risk rated "satisfactory but below investment grade." However, two banks have country risk rating systems that further differentiate "satisfactory but below investment grade" countries. This corresponds to the "best practice" recommended by RMA for borrower and facility credit risk categories. (The process of using narrower risk rating categories is referred to as increasing the "granulation.")

Country risk ratings typically supersede credit ratings. However, at one bank this is true only if the rating is rated "watch" or worse (i.e., a facility in a "pass" rated country would stand on its own credit rating merit). Generally, banks' country risk ratings automatically also become the commercial credit risk rating for external debt obligations of national, state, and provincial government agencies, and for government-majority owned companies (including banks). Consequently, the credit risk rating for borrowers that are headquartered and operate in a foreign country may not be higher than the country's credit risk rating.

The country risk rating frequently becomes the commercial credit risk rating for loans to private companies when a strong explicit or implicit commitment is made by the foreign government to support the repayment of its external debt obligations. Thus, a loan to a private borrower that would be rated a "B" based on its own financial strength, but may be protected by a foreign government of a "AAA" country, can also be risk rated "AAA."

However, banks appear to be less willing to upgrade a private borrower's credit rating based upon the prospect of government support for its debt repayment obligations. This reflects a recognition that domestic economic problems and political considerations may affect adversely the ability and willingness of foreign governments to honor their commitments to support private borrowers= repayment of their external debt, even when those borrowings required government approval. Banks criticized the rating agencies for assigning less severe credit ratings for the external debt obligations of some private borrowers than the credit risk rating they assigned to the country where the companies are headquartered and do most of their business.

Correlation to ICERC Ratings

Most multinational banks' country risk ratings generally correspond to ICERC ratings, despite the fact that ICERC ratings only cover transfer risk. Four banks' ratings do not correspond and one appears to be more conservative. For those that correspond, country risk rating categories are equivalent to the ICERC "Strong," "Moderately Strong," and "Weak" risk rating categories. For example "AAA" and "AA" bank ratings usually are equivalent to the ICERC "Strong" rating category.

The multinational banks like to know whether ICERC rates a country's credit as "Strong," "Moderately Strong," or "Weak." Though they may not use the ICERC rating for their own country credit risk rating, it helps them to evaluate the reasonableness of their own country risk ratings. There are more inconsistencies between bank country risk rating categories and definitions for higher risk countries (i.e., "BB" to "C", or #7 to #10) and ICERC's "OTRP," "Substandard," and "Value Impaired" rating categories.

Rating Development Process

Country risk ratings generally are assigned annually to every country where banks have more than a nominal exposure. The responsible governing unit, e.g., country risk management committee or international exposure committee, assigns country risk ratings. Recommendations for ratings come from a variety of sources, including specialized units located within the international credit department that prepare the annual country risk analyses, credit departments, and economic departments.

Multinational banks assign their own country risk ratings rather than relying on a third party source, such as a credit rating agency. Some bank senior credit managers reported that external country risk ratings for emerging market countries are often one half to a full grade too high. For example a country rated ABBB≅ by the rating agencies might be rated the equivalent of "BB" or "BB+" by the banks.

Rating Validation Process

Country risk committees often will discuss rating differences. For some banks, the Loan Review Department checks to see that country risk ratings are assigned properly to individual credit exposures, but does not validate the individual country risk ratings, because its staff lacks the necessary expertise. Other banks' Internal Audit Departments review the process used to develop the country risk ratings to confirm that the bank's policies and procedures are being followed. One bank uses country risk ratings assigned by major credit rating agencies to check the reasonableness of their own internal country risk ratings. Credit agency and bank country credit ratings are similar, but should not always be identical, because they measure risk for different types of debt obligations. Most rating agencies focus on sovereign (foreign government) debt while the banks ratings are usually meant also to cover the country credit risk inherent in commercial and industrial debt of companies headquartered and operating in that country.

Factoring in the ALLL Analysis

The multinational banks keep a higher level in their allowance for loan and lease losses (ALLL) account for facilities with higher country risk ratings. Therefore, the bank would increase its

ALLL to the extent that the country rating increases the risk rating of a facility. Banks reported that they move quickly to make special provisions to their ALLL when a change in country risk increases the potential for credit losses over the next 12 months. A few banks make an extra annual provision to their ALLL to cover country risk specifically. Exposure concentrations by country risk rating are used to determine the size of this provision.

Country Risk Exposure Limits

Summary Conclusions

X   Formal exposure limits are set annually.

X   Exposure is managed through the use of aggregate country exposure limits; however, credit and capital market exposure is not necessarily tracked jointly.

X   Aggregate and sublimits are recommended and reviewed by various levels of line-of-business or credit managers as needed and finally approved by the country risk committee.

X   Various methods are used for country limit compliance monitoring.

Formal Limits

Aggregate exposure limits for individual countries, and sublimits for specific products and business lines primarily are used by banks to manage and monitor country risk. Country exposure limits and sublimits are approved annually, but may be adjusted during the year to reflect improved new opportunities and changes in a country's risk profile. When a bank has a regional office, recommendations for limits and sublimits are reviewed by the senior regional manager and credit officer before being referred to the headquarter's country risk committee. Written policies and procedures for setting, changing, using, and monitoring compliance with those country exposures limits are found typically in a bank's credit manual(s).

Exposure Management

Multinational banks set aggregate risk exposure limits for almost every foreign country where they have credit or counterparty exposures. Some banks do not set aggregate exposure limits for "very low risk" countries, such as France, Germany, and the United Kingdom. Aggregate country exposure limits are used primarily to help manage and monitor exposures to emerging market countries. Aggregate country limits do not play a meaningful role in limiting exposures to most developed countries, because global competition already limits the available business. Banks that have both substantial capital markets (i.e., securities trading and underwriting) and credit related exposures (i.e., loans, letters of credit, and derivative contract receivables) typically set separate aggregate exposure limits for each. Separate limits are used, because the exposures are measured differently for capital markets and credit related activities. The aggregate exposure limits for a country is the lower of the maximum exposure the bank is prepared to permit for that country; or the total of the sublimits for the various products and services a bank offers to customers in that country. There can also be sublimits for local currency exposures.

In some multinational banks, aggregate exposure to a particular country is measured by adding the notional outstandings and commitments for credit facilities, the market value of derivative contracts that are Ain the money,≅ and the estimated value-at-risk for trading assets (securities and foreign exchange). The formulas used to estimate Acapital at risk≅ use a similar methodology. Thus, loans are assumed to require a fixed percent of capital based on their notional amount, but for trading account assets the fixed percent is applied against the estimated value-at-risk (VAR), which is much lower than the notional value of the trading account assets. The banks recognize that this approach to measuring country exposures (and allocating capital) strongly encourages them to conduct larger scale international capital markets activities, to a lesser extent fosters the development of derivatives business with strong foreign counterparties, and discourages foreign lending. One bank now uses estimated potential loss (assuming a payment default) rather than the notional US dollar amount to measure country risk exposure and capital at risk. The effect has been to reduce somewhat the bias against foreign lending and to enable banks to use a single comprehensive aggregate exposure limit for each country.

Foreign securities in trading accounts and foreign exchange positions are marked-to-market (usually daily). Banks believe that this captures a significant portion of the decline in value when country risk increases. The VAR approach is intended to capture the potential additional losses that might be suffered before the securities positions could be liquidated. Several banks reported that they are reviewing their VAR methodology for exposures to emerging market countries. Assumptions regarding market liquidity and the availability of hedging opportunities, though supported by prior experience, were too optimistic in light of recent events in Southeast Asia.

Limit Setting Process

Generally, aggregate country exposure limits are recommended by the international credit department, in consultation with the country managers and credit officers. Exposure limits are approved by the country risk committee, which consists of the bank=s senior executives.

Typically, the request for a country exposure sublimit for a particular product or service is developed by the local business unit manager in consultation with its senior credit officer. These requests are then reviewed and approved by the next higher level of business line management. For most banks, this is the country manager and the senior country credit officer. Final sublimit recommendations would be made by the bank=s international credit department and approved by the country risk committee. Generally, when a bank has a regional office responsible for that country, sublimit requests are reviewed and approved by the regional business managers and credit officers. Such requests would still be submitted to the country risk committee.

Limit Compliance Monitoring Process

The methods used to monitor compliance with aggregate country limits varies. Some banks use a centralized automated system to compile aggregate and business and product line exposure data for each country. A unit within the headquarters credit department would monitor the limits and report to the headquarters country risk committee. In another case, compliance with country business and product line sublimits is monitored by both the country credit officers and a unit within the headquarters credit department.

Approval of excess usage of country limits and sublimits is usually the responsibility of the headquarters' country risk committee. Authority to approve small or temporary overages can be delegated to the international credit department and may be delegated further to senior country credit officers or the senior regional manager and credit officer (if the bank has a regional office).

The banks= boards of directors are familiar with the limit structure; however, most do not receive formal limit exception information. Reporting varies as follows: one bank reports all country limits and exposures each quarter; another bank reports all country limits and exposures each month; one bank obtains annual board approval of its country exposure limits; and another bank obtains annual board approval for the annual Apotential loss≅ exposure limit that may be incurred for any non-OECD country. The boards of directors are usually advised of the bank=s exposure limits and usage for countries where potential problems are anticipated.

Aggregate country exposure limits and business and product line sublimits are communicated widely to international business line and credit officers at the country, regional, and headquarters level. Country managers and credit officers submit weekly, monthly, and quarterly exposure reports to the headquarters business units, its international department, and its credit department. The monthly reports include a comparison of actual and planned exposures. The quarterly reports typically include projected exposures for the balance of the year.

Marketing Strategies and Risk Tolerances

Summary Conclusions

X   Marketing strategies and risk tolerances are established mostly by line and/or division management and approved by a high level country risk management or loan committee.

X   Risk tolerances are recommended primarily by line management and approved by a high level committee.   The methodologies used in the establishment of risk tolerances vary from bank-to-bank.

Most multinational banks manage marketing strategies and risk tolerances on a global line-of-business basis. At one bank, the primary source of recommendations for marketing strategies and risk tolerances depends on the business line and country. Foreign marketing strategies at another bank are set by the division and local management. Local lending is governed by the bank=s global relationship and emerging markets management groups. In another bank, the line management (country managers) recommends limits and strategies and manages risk locally. For another multinational bank, the international credit committee and senior management approve foreign marketing strategies and credit/counterparty risk tolerances. Historically, this bank has had only one general line of business in foreign countries.

Another bank employs a process whereby bank officers cannot transact business in a foreign country without first having insider knowledge of country practices via an established branch or representative office. They also try to hire local people that are well connected within the country, highly experienced and knowledgeable of local companies, accounting practices, legal requirements, and government policies. This bank does not like to make cross-border term loans.
They watch currency values and transferability closely. Another bank=s strategy and risk tolerances are established by line management and approved by the board annually. This bank=s strategy is focused primarily on trade finance activities, and they will not extend direct sovereign exposure.

During the country risk limits setting process at another bank, country managers develop detailed country marketing and risk management strategies. Those documents are summarized into two pages and presented to the country risk management committee. At one additional bank, the foreign marketing strategies are established by line management. Risk tolerances are recommended by line management, but approved by the bank=s executive risk management committee based upon recommendations from another large corporate credit committee.

Regional Banks

Country Risk Management Process

Summary Conclusions

X   Most of the regional banks have formal, centralized processes that cover the management of country risk. Only one bank has a process that is not the direct responsibility of a senior management committee.

X   All but one of the regional banks have a formal country risk reporting mechanism. Most of these banks' country risk management groups, report at varying degrees, to the board of directors.

X   In all of the regional banks transfer risk is integrated in some manner with the credit risk or loan approval processes bank-wide, rather than treated as an independent risk.

X   Regional banks have established country risk rating systems, which in some but not all cases, correspond to their overall commercial credit risk ratings.

X   None of the banks integrate the country risk management process with the market risk management function.

Responsibility for the Process

The country risk management processes of the regional banks are centralized and integrated generally in some manner with the credit risk or loan approval process bank-wide. Most of the banks, except one, have a formal senior management committee that is responsible for the country risk management process, either directly or indirectly, through a separate country risk committee that reports to the overall credit risk committee. In one bank, the country risk committee is empowered to make all risk policy decisions that relate to any business activity outside the U.S. The committee is made up mostly of senior officers with such titles as: chief credit officer, chief international credit officer, country risk manager/analyst, and managing directors of commercial banking and global marketing.

All of the regional banks have experienced management teams with the background and skills necessary to control this area of risk. In most cases, these banks are involved primarily in trade finance activities. However, one bank has considerable experience in sovereign and foreign commercial syndicated lending activity.

Reporting Mechanism and Monitoring

The majority of the regional banks report country risk exposure regularly to the board of directors, while a few banks provide that information only to the chief credit officer. However, in general, the level of detail of country risk exposure information contained in the board of directors' reports is unclear. There is little evidence that formal presentations on country risk are made to the board. One bank has not established a formal reporting mechanism to the board or senior management. Reporting is done on an ad hoc basis. However, exposures in two of the bank's subsidiaries are reported to the board regularly.

The U.S. banks that are wholly owned by foreign banks have adopted the parent bank's country risk management processes. However, these U.S. banks report their exposures to their own boards of directors as well as that of the parent bank. Furthermore, the boards of these foreign owned U.S. banks are directly responsible for the exposures booked in the U.S. Thus, although the country risk management policies of the foreign owned U.S. banks emanate from the parent bank, the U.S. banks appear to have proper independence and governance over country risk exposures under their own responsibility.

It appears that information on country risk concentrations and/or exceptions to the banks' country risk limits is being reported to the boards of directors in at least half of the regional banks.

Country Risk Analysis Process

Summary Conclusions

X   All of the regional banks have a country risk analysis process.

X   Most country risk analyses are performed internally by the banks' economic divisions. They incorporate rating agencies' analyses into their process.

X   Content of country risk analysis files differs between banks. There appears to be no common standards for the information required to be maintained.

X   In general, information from the country risk analysis process appears to be widely disseminated within the banks.

Formal Process

In most of the regional banks surveyed, country risk analyses are prepared by their internal economic research departments. However, two banks rely on country risk analyses that are prepared by their foreign parent banks. Most banks incorporate externally prepared rating agency analyses into their internal processes, but they do not rely on them exclusively. In addition to information received from the rating agencies, one bank uses externally prepared economic research data.

The depth, or level of detail contained in the banks' country risk analyses range from minimal to detailed. In two banks, the depth of analysis is a function of the specific country and its current rating, or the banks' existing or proposed exposure limit for the country. Information on the frequency of reviews was collected at only three of the banks. One of them indicated that they conduct quarterly reviews. The other two perform annual reviews.

Information Requirements

Three regional banks have broadly outlined information that should be found in their country risk files. Some basic information found in their files includes country analyses (internal and/or external), exposure data, publications, news reports from newspapers and the Internet, and other country related data. One bank is still creating its country risk management process, while another does not have file standards and relies instead on the country risk analysis process (and presumably documentation) at its foreign parent bank.

Although two banks indicated that they routinely compared their internally assigned country risk ratings with either ICERC or other external ratings, none of the regional banks have any type of formal due diligence process to reconcile internally and externally assigned country risk ratings.

Communication of Analysis/Results

Generally, country risk analyses are disseminated widely in the regional banks. In two banks, the data is incorporated directly into the banks' loan policy. In two other banks, country risk information is made available on the bank's computer system.

Country Risk Rating Process

Summary Conclusions

X   In the regional banks, country risk is defined generally to encompass a broader spectrum of risks than transfer risk, although transfer risk is an important component.

X   Types of exposure covered by country risk ratings vary considerably because of the wide variety of business activities conducted offshore by the regional banks.

X Strong correlation exists between country risk rating and credit rating categories, particularly at the level of classified assets.

X The country risk ratings of most regional banks correspond with ICERC ratings.

X Typically, a senior credit committee or the board of directors assigns country risk ratings.

X There is no independent validation of the country risk rating process at most of the regional banks.

X In assessing ALLL adequacy, most regional banks use their respective commercial credit risk rating and reserve allocation methodologies.

Formal Risk Rating Process

The regional banks assign ratings for countries in which they are currently doing business. None of the banks exclude any countries from this process. Several banks risk rate countries proactively based on potential strategic initiatives.

One bank's risk ratings reflect the level of a country's risk of an event when it is unable to honor its foreign currency denominated obligations. Countries are rated in tiers to conform with the commercial grading system. The overall country risk rating normally will be the lower of the country risk rating or the rating of the foreign borrower. Rating tiers are determined based on ICERC country risk rating definitions, external rating agencies, economic indicators and credit criteria, and political and economic developments in a country.

Covered Types of Risk

Most of the regional banks define country risk to encompass a broader spectrum of risks than transfer risk, although transfer risk is considered to be an important component in the overall country risk evaluation by all banks. Banks typically include economic, political, social, and local regulatory considerations in the broader definition of country risk. One bank, however, reports making the country risk evaluation solely on the basis of transfer risk.

Covered Types of Exposures and Products

Generally, most of the regional banks' country risk ratings apply to almost all direct and indirect exposures. The covered types of exposure generally include:

X Direct lending.

X   Money market activities.
X   Other investments.
X   Letters of credit.
X   Counterparty credit risk.
X   Trade finance.
X   Investments.

Integration of Country and Commercial Risk

For most of the regional banks, there is a strong correlation between country risk ratings and commercial credit rating categories, particularly at the level of classified assets. However, one bank's country risk ratings are separate with no clear correlation. All banks assign the more severe rating, either credit or country, to monitor asset quality.

All credit exposures are factored into each institution's determination of the adequacy of the allowance for credit losses. None of the regional banks, however, additionally factor in aggregate cross-border exposures or exposures to non-OTRP/classified countries as a separate component of allowance for loan and lease losses.

Correlation to ICERC Ratings

Although most regional banks' commercial risk rating systems appear to correspond with ICERC ratings, the direct correlations are unclear. One bank includes the ICERC ratings in its risk rating system database. Another bank prefers to assign country risk ratings independently without considering ICERC ratings. Another bank's country risk rating policy discusses ICERC's risk rating terminology and the focus on "transfer risk." However, transfer risk is reflected as a sub-category of economic risk, which is a sub-category of country risk.

Ratings Development Process

The responsibility for assigning country risk ratings typically resides with a senior credit committee or the board of directors. Input and recommendations on the risk ratings come from various sources. In half of the regional banks, the economics department drives or assists in the process. Line departments usually are solicited for additional input or validation.

Most regional banks review country risk ratings from external rating agencies and from ICERC to confirm their views. Several foreign-owned banks also receive the opinions of their parent banks on country risk issues. Those views are considered, but the foreign-owned banks are responsible independently for the ratings and exposure levels, although they are balanced within the global bank structure.

Ratings Validation Processes

In general, the regional banks' country risk ratings are validated independently by either a loan review department or country risk committee. In addition, external-sourced country risk ratings, including ICERC ratings, are used to check the reasonableness of the internal risk ratings.

Factoring in the ALLL Analysis

All regional banks factor country risk into their allowance for loan and lease loss (ALLL) analysis. However, the methodologies vary. At one bank, country risk ratings drive commercial credit risk ratings, and the credit risk formula is applied in ALLL evaluations. In four other banks, all loans (domestic and international) are included in the same risk rating system and are factored into the ALLL analysis.

Country Risk Portfolio Management/Risk Limit Systems

Summary Conclusions

X   All but one regional bank applies their country exposure limits to the broader definition of country risk.

X   In most of the banks, the maximum level of exposure permitted for any given country is a function of the assigned country risk rating.

X   A variety of approaches exist in setting limits.

X   Most regional banks have a mechanism for reviewing concentrations and/or exceptions to their country risk limits.

Formal Limits

In most of the regional banks, the exposure limit for a particular country applies to all types of exposure. However, exceptions to this general rule were noted in four banks, which have excluded, or established separate limits, for one or more of the following types of exposure: foreign exchange, the investment portfolio, settlement risk, or locally funded indigenous exposures.

Some form of country risk sublimits exist in more than half of the regional banks, where separate limits for maturities over one year are most frequent. Although none of the banks have established separate, formal limits for regional concentrations of risk, several consider regional concentrations in their country-by-country limit setting process.

Exposure Measurement and Limit Setting Process

The basis for setting country risk exposure limits varies among the regional banks. In most of the banks, the maximum level of exposure permitted for any country is a function of the assigned country risk rating. In two banks, however, the setting of exposure limits involves a more complex calculation that considers separate ratings of other, more discrete factors, such as the economy, country size, and financial sophistication. None of the banks make any attempt to factor covariance into their limit setting process. Country exposure limits in the remaining six regional banks are all expressed as a percent of the bank's capital based on the risk rating.

In most of the regional banks, the limit setting process is an annual exercise (subject to monthly or ongoing reviews in some banks). In addition to information from the country risk analysis process, proposed country limits usually reflect a consideration of their marketing strategy and customer needs. Depending on the bank, country risk limits may be approved by the chief credit officer, a risk management committee, the bank president, or the board of directors. One bank's limits are approved on a sliding scale based on size. The lowest approval authority is at the group manager level, followed by the department committee, division executive, and other executive level officers.

Most of the regional banks' country risk limits are based on a certain percentage of capital. For example, a country rated "1" could have a maximum exposure of up to 15 percent of capital when a country rated "5" is limited to a maximum of 1 percent of capital. This process gets more complex in grades "3-5" when risk indicators (+ or -) are employed with limit implications (leave a maximum allowed or reduce to a lower level) pre-assigned.

Limit Compliance Monitoring Process

Most of the regional banks have a mechanism for reviewing concentrations and/or exceptions to their country risk limits. One bank's policy limits and exposure exceptions are reported to an executive level committee. Others require that exceptions be approved by senior officers. Generally, the limit compliance reviews are performed at least monthly.

Two regional banks have established a formal contingency or exit plan for dealing with deteriorating country risk situations. However, most banks indicate that their normal monitoring procedures enable them to deal with such situations through risk rating downgrades, shortening of tenors, freezing of unused lines, and other exposure reduction strategies.

Marketing Strategies and Risk Tolerances

Summary Conclusions

X   In most of the regional banks, marketing strategies are established by line management and approved by the bank's board of directors or a board committee.

X   Risk tolerances are recommended mostly by line management or a loan committee and approved by the boards of regional banks.

X   Management of marketing strategies varies from bank to bank.

In most of the regional banks, marketing strategies are established by line management and approved by the bank's board of directors or a board committee. At one bank, marketing strategies and risk tolerances are developed by line management and approved by a board committee. In another bank, before any foreign markets are approved for business transactions, the specific bank area must submit a formal request detailing the rationale for conducting business in a country. One bank, fairly new to international lending, is establishing a country risk management process. Marketing strategies and risk tolerances for two banks are set by a loan committee or international committee and approved by the boards of directors.

In one bank, marketing strategies are managed centrally. Another bank's marketing strategy is managed on a regional basis (e.g., Latin America, EMEA, Asia, Middle East). Only two banks manage marketing strategies on a global line-of-business basis.

Small Banks

Country Risk Management Process

Summary Conclusions

X   All of the small banks have developed formal country risk management programs and use a centralized country risk management approach.

X   In all but two instances, the small banks have adopted formal written country risk management policies that are board-approved.

X   All of the small banks have adopted formal internal tracking and reporting mechanisms.

X   The small banks are staffed with experienced managers and support staffs that are necessary to manage country risk.

Responsibility for the Process

Most of the small banks control the country risk management process through a centralized, formal international department with oversight provided by a board-appointed committee. In most of the small banks, responsibility for management of country risk is held by the senior international department executive officer. In one bank, such responsibility rests with the senior credit officer, and in another, the chairman of the board (who is also a principal owner and an active bank officer) is the responsible official.

All of the small banks have provided for a level of expertise necessary to manage country risk properly. The banks are staffed with experienced professional managers and support staffs. This process is integrated with the overall credit risk management functions in all cases.

Reporting Mechanism and Monitoring

Senior international department management officials provide regular reports to other senior bank officials, oversight committees, and their board of directors. Most of the banks have a committee designated to monitor and provide oversight over international functions on behalf of the board of directors, normally on a monthly basis. In most instances, the senior international department executive manager reports directly to the responsible oversight committee with subsequent formal reports also presented directly to the board of directors at least quarterly.

Reports presented to the boards of directors most typically include:

X   Recommended country exposure limits (for board of directors approval or ratification).
X   A summary of the bank's exposure levels by country.
X   Credit reports, including lines of credit for approval or ratification.
X   Problem accounts for information purposes and/or action, as necessary.
X   Minutes that document oversight committee actions.

In many of the small banks, the senior international department managers provide periodic briefings to their board of directors regarding recommended international activities. The information given to the various committees and boards of directors serves a dual function by providing both general information and a formal mechanism for the decision-making process. Country risk briefings most often include information that may relate to and/or affect business strategies, recommendations for country limits, and problems as they are anticipated or noted relating to both country risk and credit. In two banks, the persons responsible for country risk management also serve as bank directors, thereby providing for increased opportunities to inform their boards of directors.

Policy and Procedures

In most of the small banks, the country risk management policies have been combined into the general credit policy, and country risk issues are addressed adequately. Additionally, most of the banks have adopted formal internal tracking and reporting mechanisms. These systems provide a means of maintaining control over international activities and ensuring compliance with established policies and procedures. Although two banks have not adopted separate formal country risk policies, they have internal procedures to manage and control country risk exposures.

Staffing and Organization

In most of the small banks, international functions originate through a formally established international banking department headed by an experienced senior executive officer. Those departments report to a board-appointed oversight committee. This committee may be limited to international activities exclusively or be responsible for other bank activities, such as a general credit committee or investment committee. In one bank, the business plan is geared substantially to international activities. In another bank, the business philosophy has changed recently to the point that its board has applied to regulatory authorities to become a wholesale international bank.

Support officers typically function in the capacity of account officers. Those officers are most often assigned countries or geographic regions of individual responsibility. One larger bank has allowed the international department to include its own credit department, which provides both credit and country analysis services. In other banks, the credit staff provides support to both domestic and international lending functions.

Country Risk Analysis Requirements

Summary Conclusions

X   All of the small banks have adopted a formal country risk analysis process, although the degree of formality varies.

X   Most of the small banks prepare their own country analysis reports at least annually and monitor certain countries continuously.

X   Information maintained in country files include several varieties of reference materials that document economic trends, the socio-political environment, and the country's access to capital markets.

X   Management disseminates selected country risk information to appropriate staff members on a need-to-know basis.

Formal Process

All but one of the small banks maintain current country files that serve as reference sources for international department staff and other bank management officials. These files represent one of the more important country risk management tools. Current intelligence data becomes useful to management to determine the markets to enter, or whether a market is feasible for future business. The data maintained in the files also ultimately proves to be of benefit when used in establishing country limits. In the one bank where formal country files are not maintained, management is knowledgeable of major issues that may affect the country risk area. Additionally, that same bank also prepares and maintains country studies in a centralized location.

The majority of the small banks prepare their own country analysis reports at least annually and monitor the countries continuously. One of the banks limits internally prepared reports (prepared on a semi-annual basis) to three of its primary markets and relies on external ratings for the other analysis reports. Two of the banks depend totally on the services of an external independent rating service. The analysis reports, regardless of origin, are detailed. External rating services also are used by the majority of the other banks as an additional source of information. For instance, two of the banks subscribe to the external ratings services. All of this material provides substantial information into the banks' formal country risk analysis process.

Information Requirements

Materials in small banks' country files generally include:

X   Internal and external country analysis reports.

X   Business periodicals.

X   Various types of foreign government publications.

X   Information obtained from correspondent bank clients (e.g., annual reports).

X   Management trip memoranda.

X   Documentation of important committee and board of directors actions that affect a given country strategy.

X   Other information deemed pertinent.

Additionally, most of the banks maintain other reference materials that are typically kept separate from the formal country file, such as rating information and updates provided by external rating services. Also, various periodicals are maintained for management's use. Senior management of the majority of the banks provide for a degree of due diligence over the country risk analysis process by reconciling ratings disparities between internal and external sources prior to board of directors' review.

Communication of Analysis/Results

The small banks generally provide for continuous communications, both internally and externally. Country risk considerations are communicated formally and internally to higher management levels. Additionally, external communication is maintained by the applicable banks with their respective foreign domiciled offices operated either directly by the bank or through affiliated institutions and representatives. Also, external communication, which normally consists of a given central bank and/or banking supervisory authority, is maintained with the various sovereign bank regulatory authorities. Intelligence gained through this process is incorporated into the daily country risk management process, including the planning and decision-making processes.

Three of the small banks limit the material distributed to the country risk analysis reports. The other banks commonly disseminate to applicable staff other selected information that in addition to the country analysis reports ultimately becomes part of an active country file. Line officers have access to country files and other reference materials, as necessary.

Country Risk Rating Process

Summary Conclusions

X   All of the small banks have adopted a process for determining the degree of country risk in their respective markets.

X   Generally, all risk rating processes cover a broad definition of country risk. Transfer risk is a consideration within this framework.

X   The country risk rating process, whether internally maintained or provided by an independent outside servicer, covers all types of exposures, including both funded and unfunded transactions.

X   Most of the small banks that have adopted country risk rating systems have done so for both credit risk and country risk.

X   In most of the banks, internal risk rating definitions can be correlated to ICERC ratings.

X   Senior management officials are responsible mostly for making recommendations on the assignment of country risk ratings.

X   Small banks do not maintain internal audit and/or loan review staffs that possess necessary knowledge and experience to validate country ratings.

X   In assessing ALLL adequacy, small banks use their respective commercial credit risk rating and reserve allocation methodologies.

Formal Risk Rating Process

Four banks have adopted their own internal country risk rating processes. Two other banks rely on external country risk rating services, but may not necessarily be bound to the rating assigned. In the last case, the bank uses external ratings for reference purposes. All of the banks also reference ICERC ratings in their internal country risk management procedures.

Covered Types of Risk

The small banks' country risk rating processes measure economic, political, social, and credit risks that may affect target markets. However, most of the small banks consider credit risk to be a higher priority than transfer risk.

Covered Types of Exposures and Products

The small banks almost exclusively provide trade and trade-related financing to correspondent banks. Also, loans are made to private banking customers, mostly on a secured basis. Examples of exposures and products included are all types of loans, bankers acceptances, unfunded portions of formal (committed) lines of credit, and letters of credit. Investment transactions, mostly in the form of placements, are also covered in some instances.

Integration of Country and Commercial Risk

Although most of the small banks' country risk rating systems encompass both credit and country risks, their processes are somewhat different. One bank uses an internal risk rating process that encompasses both credit risk ratings and country risk ratings. The ultimate rating assigned is limited at best to the ICERC rating. Another bank uses separate rating processes that combine quantitative and qualitative indicators. The composite rating is determined based on key economic statistics, political climate, country fiscal and monetary policies, and the ICERC and a major rating service ratings. A third bank does not use an internal country risk rating system, but relies on external analysis and ICERC ratings. This bank does use its own separate commercial credit rating process with ultimate credit ratings being limited by the ICERC country rating (e.g., the ICERC rating establishes a ceiling). A fourth bank has provided for separate rating processes; however, the credit rating is affected directly by the country rating (lower country ratings result in lower credit ratings).

Correlation to ICERC Ratings

Some of the small banks have adopted the same rating terminology and definitions as used by ICERC. Two of the banks defer their ratings to the ICERC ratings, while the other banks factor the ICERC rating into their respective rating processes. The banks that defer to ICERC do so to ensure that they identify risks in accordance with the regulatory process.

The internally assigned country risk ratings typically follow a tiered scheme that include ratings categories that run from "low risk" to "high risk" (in most cases by using a numerical scale running from "1" [low risk] to "8" [highest risk] or an alpha scale starting with "A" running through "D"). When numerical ratings are assigned, the numbers correlate to the following ICERC definitions: numbers "1" through "4" represent acceptable risk categories (or equivalent to "strong" through "weak"), "5" generally equates to "Other Transfer Risk Problem," "6" equates to "Substandard," "7" equates to "Value Impaired," and finally, "8" equates to "Loss." In one instance, the bank merely assigns a "pass" or "no pass" rating to a given country, indicating that the bank will extend credit only in a country rated as a "pass" and vice versa.

Rating Development Process

In the small banks that have their own country risk analysis programs, the country analyst makes the initial recommendation for an assigned rating for both country and credit risk. The recommended rating is reviewed by senior executive international department management and by an oversight committee. The banks' boards of directors are the final approving authority in most cases.

Rating Validation Process

In general, the small banks do not maintain internal audit and/or loan review staff that possess the appropriate knowledge and/or experience to serve as a validation tool for country ratings. In most cases, credit risk ratings assigned by account officers for individual credits receive subsequent review (for general validation purposes) by the loan review process. However, for country risk ratings, the only review that may take place is by senior international executive managers. However, their review is limited to questioning the country risk ratings based on their own experiences and sources of information before they are submitted to bank-wide management. Nonetheless, this particular review process does provide some validation by allowing the managers to question ratings prior to submission to higher authorities.

Factoring in the ALLL Analysis

In assessing the adequacy of the allowance for loan and lease losses (ALLL) for country risk exposures, the small banks use their respective commercial credit risk rating and reserve allocation methodologies. The banks have adopted the interagency policy for loan loss reserve adequacy that incorporates considerations for transfer risk adjustments. However, the nature of the transactions, which mostly include short-term trade and trade-related credits, generally negates the need for significant transfer risk or credit risk reserve allocations. Credits are assessed on their own respective merits. At least one small bank factors in credits assigned to the ICERC "Other Transfer Risk Problem" category in determining allowance provision requirements. Historically, the banks have made ATRR provisions in accordance with regulatory requirements.

Country Risk Limit System

Summary Conclusions

X   All of the small banks have established processes for setting country risk limits; however, the degree of formality varies in each instance.

X   Country limits relate to the broader definition of country risk that encompasses transfer risk.

X   Exposures of all types are included in the exposure management process. Exposure levels are monitored and managed by tracking the net exposure levels by country compared with outstanding levels of the banks' Tier 1 capital.

X   Most of the small banks have adopted a formal process to set country limits that are based on a percentage of Tier 1 capital. Half of the banks have not established limits for low risk countries.

X   Many of the small banks have established formal policy guidance to address limit exception procedures.

Formal Limits

Country risk limits are established only when the particular bank has determined that business opportunities either exist or will exist. In some cases, when a bank may have only an occasional transaction (usually representing a customer accommodation), it may not perform a formal country risk evaluation or establish a country limit. Rather, the specific transactions are approved on a case-by-case basis. Additionally, half of the banks have not established country limits for "low risk" countries such as Germany, France, and the United Kingdom.

Country risk limits are expressed most often in terms of a maximum aggregate dollar volume of net exposure per country. Net exposure is basically referred to as the amount of outstanding transactions after applying cross-border guarantees and/or collateral. In at least three of the banks, maximum country risk limits are expressed as a percentage of Tier 1 capital. In any event, management information exposure reports provided to all levels of bank management most often include both aggregate gross exposure (prior to adjustments for guarantees and/or collateral) and net exposure in terms of dollar volume, as well as expressed as a percentage of Tier 1 capital.

Some banks use the stated limits as maximum ceilings with the actual levels of outstanding net exposure maintained at much lower levels. This particular process is often a function of available or potential business. Maximum limits are sometimes set at higher levels, based on risk analysis procedures, to allow for future business development opportunities. Some other banks have approved individual credit lines that, when aggregated within a given country, exceed the maximum country risk limit for that country. Management must track outstandings carefully in those cases to ensure compliance with established maximum country limits. This process allows management to take advantage of an available country limit volume by balancing the outstandings of customer credit lines against that country limit. For example, when one credit line is inactive, or only partially active, the bank can take advantage of a larger customer base of approved credit lines.

Country limits relate in all cases to the broader definition of country risk, which also encompasses transfer risk. Also included in the country risk definition are political, economic, and social risks. Credit risk is also considered as the banks integrate credit risk into country risk analysis. The premise for doing this is that the type of credit risk incurred likely will have a direct bearing on country risk considerations (particularly transfer risk). This is especially true when the banks are financing activities critical to the ongoing survival of the country or that involve the major banks within a given country.

In general, credits that are guaranteed by the U.S. government (as in the case of the U.S. Export Import Bank) or secured by cash, marketable securities, or U.S. based real estate do not get applied against the limits. In one bank, separate "dollar volume" country limits are approved for the bank and its Latin American subsidiary.

Only three of the small banks have established formal country risk sublimits. One bank has sublimits that have been established based on tiered maturities (e.g., short-term and medium term) of trade and trade-related transactions. A second bank has sublimits only for its four primary markets. The third bank has established sublimits only for one country, its primary target market. Those banks have established sublimits by type of exposure (e.g., funded, unfunded, letters of credit, bankers acceptances) on a borrower specific basis.

While the majority of the banks do not establish regional concentration limits, all of them are cognizant of exposures by geographic areas. All of the banks regularly produce tracking reports used by management to monitor exposure levels and trends. Necessary adjustments to outstanding exposures often are made to correct for high concentrations within a given country or a group of countries located in a specific region.

Exposure Management

All types of exposure, both funded and unfunded, are included by the small banks in the exposure management process. Exposure management normally begins with the country risk analysis process and the establishment of country limits (on a country-by-country basis). Exposure levels are monitored and managed by tracking the net exposure levels by country compared with outstanding levels of the bank's Tier 1 capital.

Access to information relating to the banks' international activities has improved over the past few years. Historically, small banks sometimes found analytical information difficult to obtain. The frequency and timeliness of receiving data from small bank clients has also improved significantly. The banks have access daily to economic, political, and social information relating to a given country through advanced technology, including the Internet. Many Internet sites provide analysts and managers with substantial volumes of various types of data.

Foreign supervisory authorities are also being more cooperative in providing statistical information relating to economic and financial trends. The same sources also make available information on their respective banking systems, including data relating to specific banks operating within their respective country. Bank clients provide increased access to financial information on a more timely basis. The small U.S. banks are not only in a position to obtain annual statements, but also are beginning to receive interim financial statements. Data provided for review is also becoming more detailed and reliable as many of the countries have begun to adopt more disclosure requirements and more formal accounting guidelines.

None of the small banks consider covariance of country risk exposures when establishing country risk limits.

Limit Setting Process

The majority of the small banks have adopted a formal process to set country limits. In general, limits are established by reviewing periodically foreign credit markets, through prepared or acquired country studies, internal and external country ratings, current or anticipated foreign credit opportunities, and Tier 1 capital levels. One of the banks sets its limits informally, but has established exposure caps for both developed country and lesser-developed country transactions.

Line management recommends or reviews most country limits, and all banks require formal board approval before limits are established formally. Those limits generally are reviewed and approved at least annually. Two of the banks review their respective country limits quarterly along with updated country risk data from outside rating services. In each case, limits represent guidance levels; the banks may withdraw or reduce the country limits as necessary. Those actions normally require board of director approval, although senior management officials normally can temporarily suspend or reduce limits in emergencies.

Limit Compliance Monitoring Process

Concentration levels, as well as all exposures, are reviewed by senior management, board appointed oversight committees, and the board of directors. Senior executive management is responsible typically for ensuring that the bank remains within established country limits. Detailed management reports of outstanding exposures are prepared regularly by most banks to assist in the monitoring and management process. Reports submitted at the committee and/or board of directors level vary from disclosing only concentrations, to disclosing fully all exposures and other related matters. Reports are submitted through the management chain (senior international management, the oversight committee, and finally the board of directors) at least quarterly. Most banks provide monthly reports. Most management reports have been regarded historically by examining personnel as generally sufficient.

The majority of the small banks formally review country limits at least annually, in conjunction with the updated country risk analysis process. Two banks update the country limit approvals quarterly. All of the banks have the latitude to make limit adjustments as needed (driven primarily by business opportunities and/or country developments). At least two of the banks also conduct annual credit line reviews in conjunction with the country risk updates and country limit approval process.

Many of the small banks have established formal policy guidance to address limit exception procedures. The typical policy requirement dictates that country limit exceptions be documented and approved properly. Reports are submitted through the management chain for review and ultimate ratification by the board of directors. File documentation is maintained to document each exception, including the basis of the limit exception, as well as the approval and review process. Country limit exceptions historically have been granted on a temporary basis, with appropriate justification and approval documented.

Although only two banks have adopted formal written contingency plans (e.g.,"exit plans"), all of the banks know the strategic actions necessary to protect their interests. This fact has been demonstrated especially throughout the banks' target markets. At most small banks, senior international officials can take immediate action in emergencies to protect the banks' interests. Such actions typically include temporary suspension or reduction of country limit authorizations. Subsequent transactions are handled on a case-by-case basis. Any actions taken are reported subsequently to bank-wide senior managers and are reviewed ultimately by the board of directors.

Marketing Strategies and Risk Tolerances

Summary Conclusions

X   The majority of the small banks' marketing strategies start with formal corporate strategic plans that establish the initial basis for marketing efforts.

X   The key marketing strategy most commonly used in the case of the small banks is their established client network, mainly correspondent banks.

X   Senior line management has influence over risk tolerances, but the ultimate decisions relating to the policies rest at higher levels, including committee review and board approval.

The majority of the small banks' marketing strategies start with formal corporate strategic plans that establish the initial basis for marketing efforts. Senior management officials implement marketing strategies to meet the established corporate strategic goals. The process is influenced greatly by the volume of available business from each identified potential market area. Also, competition is a driving force, and sometimes a limiting one. Senior management has significant influence over both marketing strategies and risk tolerances. Normally, those efforts are coordinated by senior management in conjunction with the aid of staff input.

Only one bank uses a formal marketing division for marketing support. The other banks handle marketing programs more informally. The key marketing strategy most commonly noted in the case of the small banks is using their established client network, mainly correspondent banks. The banks make contact with potential clients, often through referred introductions, by actually traveling to the potential client's home country for face-to-face marketing similar to domestic call programs.

The types of business activity financed by the banks often reduces the need for substantial marketing efforts. The majority of the small bank business relates to trade and trade-related transactions through well established correspondent bank networks. The main consideration is the ability of the banks to meet the needs of the client banks. Client banks have expected consistently more favorable financing terms, including lower rates, longer tenors, and lower (or no) compensating deposit balance requirements. To date, the banks have maintained underwriting programs that are mindful of the risks associated with granting the desired favorable terms. Senior line management also has influence over risk tolerances, but the ultimate decisions relating to the policies rest at higher levels, including committee review and board approval.

Prior to implementing a new product or service (hereafter referred to as product), all of the banks conduct market research, including research on country risk issues that may likely affect the particular product under consideration and the corresponding degree of existing or potential market interest. In the past, new products have been implemented cautiously. Net exposures are allowed to build in increments to provide for steady growth. This process also facilitates proper exposure management.

Attachment

COUNTRY RISK MANAGEMENT PROCESSES QUESTIONNAIRE
DATA COLLECTION PROJECT

September 1997

Instructions to ICERC Examiners:

The bank regulatory agencies wish to review the country risk management processes currently used by U.S. banks to verify its information on these processes. Examiners from the OCC, Federal Reserve, and FDIC will gather information on the country risk management processes of those banks that are involved routinely in the ICERC country risk discussions. To guide the information gathering exercise, a set of questions on various areas of country risk management is attached.

Most of the information requested in the attached questions probably is known already to the examiners based on their current understanding of the banks' country risk management processes or is available through recent examination activities. Recourse to appropriate risk management officers in the banks may be necessary when information gaps exist. Examiners might obtain needed additional information during their discussions with banks prior to the Fall 1997 ICERC meeting or through regular examinations. The attached set of questions is not intended, however, as a formal questionnaire to be given to the banks.

In response to possible questions from banks about the purpose of this information gathering exercise, examiners might indicate that we are merely interested in bringing current our information on banks' country risk management processes.

Information to be Gathered by the ICERC Review Examiners:

1. **Describe the bank's Country Risk Management process.** Please provide sufficient descriptive comments on at least the following elements to give the reader a full comprehension of the Country Risk Management process.

    *   Is the process centralized or decentralized?

    *   Is the process integrated with the bank's overall credit risk and/or market risk management functions?

    *   Who is responsible for this process? Describe broadly their country risk expertise and experience.

    *   Is there a formal reporting mechanism to the bank's board of directors?

    *   Is there a formal country risk management policy? (If possible, please obtain a copy of any pertinent country risk management policies.)

    *   Where does the bank place transfer risk in the hierarchy of risks?

2. **Describe the bank's Country Risk Rating process.** Please provide sufficient descriptive comments on at least the following elements to give the reader a full comprehension of the Country Risk Rating process.

    *   Do the country risk ratings cover only transfer risk or do they cover a broader definition of country risk? If the country risk ratings cover more than transfer risk, which other risks do the ratings cover?

    *   What types of exposure receive country risk ratings? Is local currency lending exposure included? Investment portfolio exposure?

    *   How do these ratings relate to the bank's commercial rating system (e.g., does the commercial facility rating take precedence over the country risk rating)?

    *   How do these ratings correspond with the ICERC rating system, if at all?

    *   Who is responsible for assigning country risk ratings?

    *   Who independently validates these ratings (e.g., credit policy, loan review, and audit)?

- Are any countries excluded from the risk rating system? If so, explain.

- How are country risk ratings factored into the bank's ALLL analyses?

3. **Describe the bank's Country Risk Limit system.** Please provide sufficient descriptive comments on at least the following elements to give the reader a full comprehension of the Country Risk Limit system.

  - How are country risk limits set? Approved? How often are they reviewed/approved? Are the limits binding or are they merely guidelines?

  - Do the limits apply only to transfer risk or do they apply to a broader definition of country risk?

  - If the country risk limits cover more than only transfer risk, which other risks do the limits cover?

  - What types of exposure are included in and excluded from the limits (e.g., short-term trade financing, standby LC's, marketable securities, and equity investments)?

  - Are there sublimits by type of exposure?

  - Does the bank have regional concentration limits? If so, are they integrated with the bank's overall concentration management system?

  - Does the bank consider the covariance of country risk exposures when establishing country risk limits? If so, explain.

  - Are limit exceptions and/or concentrations reported to senior management and/or the board?

  - Does the bank have contingency action plans for dealing with deteriorating country risk situations?

4. **Describe the bank's Country Risk Analysis requirements.** Please provide sufficient descriptive comments on at least the following elements to give the reader a full comprehension of the Country Risk Analysis requirements.

  - Is there a formal process for maintaining country risk analysis files?

- What minimum information is required to be in country risk analysis files (e.g., current analyses, call memos, support for limit approvals, and external analysis)?

- Does the bank prepare internal country risk analysis? How detailed? How often?

- Or, does the bank rely on external analysis? If so, what are the main sources?

- Is there a "due diligence" mechanism to document agreement or disagreement with the external source?

- How is country risk analysis information communicated through the bank?

5. **Describe how bank management establishes its Marketing Strategies and Risk Tolerances for foreign exposures/markets.** Please provide sufficient descriptive comments on at least the following elements to give the reader a full comprehension of how Foreign Marketing Strategies and Risk Tolerances are established.

- Are foreign marketing strategies and risk tolerances established/managed by line management or by the Country Risk Management Department? Explain.

- Are the bank's foreign marketing strategies and risk exposures managed on a global line-of-business basis (e.g., corporate banking, middle market, and retail banking) or on a geographic or legal entity basis? Explain.

www.ingramcontent.com/pod-product-compliance
Lightning Source LLC
Chambersburg PA
CBHW052019280526
45793CB00005B/1042